CW00419071

SUR NAKED! A Fail-Proof How-to Guide to Surfing for Adults Only!

By International Bestselling Surf Author
of "The Ride Home- A Surf Novel"
Jacob Ray

Surf Naked!

Unlike other surf guides, this one wishes it could share the joy of riding a wave with every single living soul on the planet. Most guides teach you to become a clique member. You are taught to think you are a kook, then, a Barney, then, an expert asshole local. Good news: there is no social strata. No one cares. If you are interested in pleasing other surfers, don't even start surfing. Seriously. Don't. They are much more interested in themselves. If they have been surfing consistently for any amount of time, you are a nuisance to them, know your place. They will reject you, hurt your feelings, and make you clamber to no end for their affection and praise. The worst thing they do is make you worship the idea of the surf master. But, good news: there is no ideal. You can learn to surf by having the right equipment, discipline, and consistency. Basically, if you purchase the equipment and surf every single day you can and keep at it, you will get it. Surfing naked means you go without inhibition. You embody the charge.

One day, after you have embarrassed yourself, been yelled at by some douche, and gotten in everybody's way you will catch your first real ride. Then, you are hooked. The ocean will try to convince you to stay out more than you should and invariably you will meet a surf buddy who says its blown out or not worth it everyday its not perfect but you have to go anyway. Fuck them. Fuck it. If you have time and the equipment, go. Don't let other dudes convince you its not worth it. As a matter of fact, don't ask them about anything. Other surfers that aren't your friends suck. Don't talk to them. Don't engage them out of politeness. Resist that voice. If you talk to them they will instantly know you're a kook. Just resist talking to everybody when you're starting out. Surfing is the hardest, most dangerous water sport out there. Don't advertise your dangerous ignorance of that critical fact. Surfers are all narcissistic assholes, present company proudly included. Who else would risk their life to look cool like that? Suicidal narcissists. That's what it takes and who we are. If you are not cut from that raw cloth, don't buy or rent a board. Don't learn. You will just be hated and eventually someone will put you in your place or you will get hurt or hurt somebody. Surfing is an art and a sport. Like all sports, it follows you as your identity. If you see yourself as anything other than a jock-artist in the water, don't surf. You will fail. You must accept that surfing is a hardcore sport. Thinking that it is easy, mellow, relaxing, and full of long, perfect rides is false. You will curse and scream and want to break your board in half sometimes. You will literally wonder if you made a huge mistake by buying a board. You will feel so stupid sometimes when you're surfing out there because you can't catch anything, no matter what you do. Your frustrating howls and curses will fall silent on the deaf ear of the ocean. You will paddle in place ad infinitum and catch nothing. You will have days where everyone else is ripping and you suck. You will have days where no matter how hard you try, no matter how much you protest, you will not get a single ride. You will have days where you will see your life flash before your eyes. You will regret ever having thought of kidding yourself by thinking you could handle this new sport. People in the water will make you so angry you will literally want to murder them. You will embarrass yourself by screwing up and getting in the way. You will have to scurry out of there with your tail between your legs to avoid the mob. You will have times where you flake on the ocean and stop surfing and when you start back, you will suck. That's why my method is really for hardcore disciples. My system will not work if you don't manically surf. That is, you surf constantly. You relocate to a beach. You go every chance you get. You don't listen to surfers who complain about poor conditions. You go anyway. You lower expectations, knowing repetition is the mother of skill. In order to surf, you surf daily or every day you can. You get in for fifteen minutes. You get in for five hours. You go all the time. Let that be your testament. Don't brag. Don't talk about the tides and a break you frequent. Let your surfing do the talking. Watch all the videos, read all the books, buy all the stuff, but most of all: surf every chance you get. Otherwise, you cannot expect success. You are just in the way of those of us who have committed. You are the single person at the party of couples married to the ocean. You are on the fence and we bear the ring. You must ceremonially commit your life to the ocean. You must marry her, knowing she is like all women, fickle and deadly but irresistibly seductive and enigmatic. She is your mother. She nurtures you. She gives the best, most life giving milk you can imbibe and become. She is also chunky, mothered milk that tastes like salt water and death. She can suckle you to health or smother you with panic. You never know what mood she is in. She is nature, unforgiving and for survivalists only. You will curse her or you will praise her. She may or may not hear you. She may spare some but not all. Sometimes she will take you out or hurt you bad. A dude I know that surfed Mavericks in February just got his skull split on a shitty small day. He had to have plastic surgery to reconstruct his face. The tail of his board shattered on his forehead, no joke. This was a few weeks ago. Our biggest surf is in the late fall and winter but his injury happened on a blown out slop day. This friend surfed professionally. His near death experience had nothing to do with lack of skill. It was pure coincidence.

That brings me to the most important thing about surfing: you never know what your experience will be. You might read this and never touch a board. You might read this and buy a board and become a phenom. Either way, I am not liable for what these words make you do. If you follow my method, you might die the first day. I am not the ocean. I am bound to laws. One of the laws I am bound to is to warn you now that you can die anytime surfing. It might be on the best day, the smallest day, the worst day, or the biggest but it can happen. It happens in San Francisco at least ten times a year. Some surfer drowns at my beach once a month. I remember one guy they said had just surfed with great success in Costa Rica before he came to our beach in February. He died. I was in the water that day. He will never see his loved ones again. He will be the subject of great pain for his family. He is still sad out there as a ghost now, beautiful and perfect in every way. But, he is guilty of the first rule of surf safety: know and accept that as soon as you enter the ocean you are entering chaos and can die. You are willingly giving your life over to a fickle mother who may nurse or smother. You are saying goodbye to the land and gravity's normal pull. You are entering the elemental essence you mostly are made from. You can't breath it after exiting the womb but it is still you. You were once floating in the life giving essence that embodies and powers the waves who call you to them now. Read this book. Go buy a board. Surf every single chance you get and rip it up. But, for God's sake know that I am in no way liable for bad shit that might happen to you. This guide is for long term surfers. You can count on getting seriously hurt or even killed somewhere along the way. So, if you don't want to risk life and limb, return this book now. Otherwise, welcome to the closest heaven-like feeling you will ever know.

Your beach:

Where do you live?

I am in San Francisco, California, U.S.A. Where you live is CRITICAL to your surfing. You MUST research everything you can about the surf spots you are willing to travel to for this. Get on www.surfline.com. Find your local beach. Read every detail about it. If you don't have the Internet go to the beach you plan to surf. Look at it carefully and obtain whatever factual data you can about it. Be thorough. This is not a gym membership. The ocean does not care who you are or are not. You are simply a part of it, once you enter it. If you are lacking access to facts about a break, make a conservative judgement call. Are the waves small, medium, large, or death large? If they are not small or medium, you have no business being there. An easy way to judge waves for safety is nothing over your head, for the first year. You might get away with surfing a large break for the rest of your life with no problems but most likely you will get douched, hard. Don't mess with big waves. Unless you are on a deserted island with big waves and nothing else, do not try to be hardcore. You will get douched. No kidding. It is the law of Nature and has no exceptions. Where you live predetermines your success with surfing. If you are living on a lake complaining about the waves and blaming this book, don't. Move. Pack up and move to a beach. If you are in an area that has nothing but crowded beaches and you can't surf like you want to, move. Don't blame this book, the ocean, surfing, or your board. Crowds destroy concentration. You cannot learn as fast in a packed place. If you have no choice, know that you will have to pay your dues with the local assholes. They will block you out of every wave. They will glare at you. If they didn't get picked for the football team back in high school, they might go as far as to reprimand you by yelling or fighting you. Fuck those jerks. Don't let them stop you from surfing, especially if you live in that city or town and pay rent or a mortgage and property tax. Fuck them but at the same time they are your Gods. Easiest way to avoid confrontation: GET OUT OF THEIR WAY WHEN THEY ARE UP AND

RIDING! Just try to hop in when no one is there or the fewest numbers crowd the water and peaks. Go during the day during the workweek to escape the crowds. Never ever go surfing without looking at the waves first. Even if you had to travel to get there, DO NOT GET IN until you look at the waves. Know that looking at the waves can make no difference in the quality of your session. You might think it looks mellow and safe only to be paddling for dear life as an unexpected monster set rolls in and holds you down for the count. You might get in on a day that looks perfect and not get a single ride. That is surfing. It is like riding a bicycle that sometimes liquifies. You can balance on it. You know how to ride and balance yourself but sometimes your vehicle absconds with your ego. Surfing is not yours. It is a byproduct of chance and loose factors. It is a footing, graciously pardoned, by a fickle salted Queen. DO NOT try to surf without learning everything you can about the beach you plan to learn from. A good rule of thumb for the beginner/kook is: is this beach for kids, adults, beginners, and experts? Then, that is where you should learn. If you are geographically screwed and only have the beach you have, stay close to the shore. Don't go out to the big ones. You will be regarded as a nuisance and an obstacle to the local assholes. Don't brave the crowd. It detracts from your development. Surfers earn their stripes. You don't take one Karate lesson and get a black belt. You work your way up. Never lose sight of your experience level in relation to your local beach. If you don't see a bunch of teens, kids, beginners and older surfers, find another beach. If you are geographically isolated, be careful. Use common sense: if the waves look dangerous and scary from the shore, chances are they mean business. If you decide to get in and feel apprehensive, GET OUT. Do no wait around for injury. TRUST YOUR INSTINCT. If your beach is consistently deadly and frightening, move or don't try surfing. You will get hurt. I started surfing the kook beaches before moving to Ocean Beach. I live in constant fear and anxiety over surfing here. It never goes away. I drive to the beginner spots in the winter to avoid dying. I suggest you do the same. Do not let pride or ego influence your surf decisions. It will only result in injury or death. Again, this is a life and death individual water sport. Your failure or success with learning to surf depends almost entirely on where you are geographically. If you just can't get enough information about your local beach, ask the surf shop where you will have to buy surfwax. The employee will probably be a dick or obtuse with you but if they are nice buy something else if they start giving you good, detailed information. You must buy your way in to surfing. It cannot be acquired without paying the industries that engulf it. Unless you are on a deserted island and are carving a board out of wood, you will HAVE to deal with a surf shop at some point. Don't be annoying. Just get in, buy your stuff, and get out. Again, let your surfing do the talking. Surfers who sit in a shop all day bitching about their local break while detailing their trip to Bali or Hawaii last month are kooks. They are insecure narcissists who need validation. Instead of trying to match egos with them, just go surf. Those guys are the same guys who have a look on their face like they are holding a piece of shit in their mouth everywhere they go.

Ignore them. They might rip. They might be the best badass you have ever seen surf but if they ignore you or talk over your head or clown you, they are a dick, period. Don't worship them. Don't ask them the ego-stroking questions you think you should. It just makes them worse. Leave veteran surfers out of your life, in the beginning. Let them come to you, if at all. If they don't, keep surfing anyway. Don't try to ask them about boards, fins, wetsuits, waxing methods, videos, or repairs. They will just think you're a kook. They will give you a smart ass answer. Look it up yourself. I will reference every aspect of surfing in this brief book but I expect you to research things on your own. Don't blame me for shitty surf experiences if you don't finish this book and follow my method. Part of adding to my beach by teaching you how to surf properly requires that you accept responsibility for your role in your development. It is a poor carpenter who blames the tools. Don't be that guy. Get informed. Watch hours of surf video. But, know that with this sport, your success is directly proportionate to the amount of research, time, effort, and trial-and-error learning experiences

logged in. Surfing is a mind set. It is a
position in reality made up of scaly
restraint and reckless abandon. That is
why I am making you read this before
getting to the good part: how to surf.

Congratulations! Here's the technical stuff:

1. Your first board: you should get the longest, most expensive board you can afford. Good namebrands include: Channel Islands (Al Merrick), ...Lost, Anacapa (for those on a budget), FireWire, and Rusty. Surfboards come in three basic sizes: short, hybrid, and longboards. Hybrids and longboards are what you want. If you are six feet tall, get at least an eight foot long board to start with. DO NOT BUY A SHORTBOARD. You will be tempted to buy a shortboard for a lesser price but don't do it. Get a hybrid, which is a combination short and long board or just get a long board. If you are a fatass, get a longboard. If you are lazy and like to cut corners or are older, get a longboard. If you aspire to shortboard, start with a hybrid, at least a foot taller than you stand. Do not let a surf shop sales dude bilk you out of hundreds more that you can afford for a board of any size. Do not let your strange desire to impress them make you spend money you

don't have. Go to the used section first. Your first board will be a joke to you years later, after you build a real quiver. Just get something at least a foot taller than you are and wide. Narrow boards are not for you. They have a pin tail for speed. You don't need a pin tail. Pin tails look like a 'V' you want a longboard or hybrid with a rounded tail, shaped like a 'U' or a squared off tail. The tail displaces water. Different shapes are used for special waves. Buying a wide hybrid or regular longboard is your safest investment. Tails are almost always rounded or squared off. Board width affects rides also. Do not buy narrow boards with pin tails, even if they are long enough. You will get tossed over and over. Get something as wide as your shoulders across. DO NOT BUY SOFT-TOP boards for my method. They suck. They have a foamy top and do not require wax but they are too heavy and slow. Get a real surfboard to use my methods. Fins are included. Some surf shop sales dicks will try to get you to drop a hundred extra for fins. Most boards come with fins, even if they are not installed at the time of purchase. Ask them to install your fins if you are unsure about doing it yourself. If you ever install fins, screw them in just enough, too hard and you will crack your board and allow water in which is like cancer to their delicate foamy souls. Some boards are defined by their fins. The Fish is a great board to learn on. It has two fins, is thick enough to float you, and can be fine at only six inches taller than you stand. The Fish is great for surfers with smaller cars. The other fun, retro board is a Single Fin. It can be a great learning board. Find one by Al Merrick and Rob Machado. Get it a foot taller than you stand. The singular fin turns on a dime. It will toss you but not as bad as a narrow pintail will. Stay away from cheap new boards. Surfing is expensive. Be prepared to spend some money. You cannot learn as fast on crap equipment. You can cut corners on spending but in the beginning, its not worth skimping. If you are broke, get the longest board you can. Leashes are required equipment. Some badasses like to surf without them.

They look so stupid swimming to the shore after every failed ride. Get a leash for your board. Leashes should be two feet longer than your board is tall. The leash goes on your back foot, the foot closest to the tail. To attach your leash, feed a tied section of strong string through the hole near the tail end on the top or deck of your board. Once you feed the loop through, push the knotted end through the loop and pull taut. I suggest doubling up. Get two pieces of string. That way, if one snaps, you have a back up. Don't make your string too long! It needs to stop short of the rails or you risk rubbing through the glass over time. Attach the velcroed end that is opposite the ankle wrap. Don't worry about putting your leash on until you are at the water's edge. Don't strap it on and walk. You look ridiculous and the leash will trip you, over and over. Don't take it off until you exit the water. The leash should be tight around your ankle. Too tight is no good, too loose is dangerous. When your leash is loose around your ankle, it will trip you as you're popping up! If your leash gets caught on something underwater, usually a rock, don't freak out. Most leashes have a bright colored loop to yank off the velcroed ankle wrap piece. Dive down and open your eyes underwater. Look for the loop. Pull it to free your leg. Return to surface. Anytime you are in the ocean and underwater panicking, quit flailing limbs and burning oxygen, open your eyes and find up or free yourself from the stuck leash. To carry your board, turn the bottom towards your body or you will get wax all over your clothes. Always carry the board nose first, tucked under your arm with the bottom against your body and fins behind you. Why? If you carry your board fins forward and a strong enough breeze comes along, it will jam your fins into you. Ouch. Wrap the leash around the end of the board and use the velcro to secure it. Don't wrap too tight! You will leave indentions in your rails! To navigate around inside your home with surf boards, always glance at both ends before and during moving the board. Don't walk a board from one place to another without robotically monitoring the nose and tail every step you take. You will ding it on everything if you muscle it around. Watch the ends as you move with it. Dings need to be fixed. A ding is a malignant tumor on your board. It is allowing water into the internal foam beneath the glass. Water is insidious. It goes to the wooden stringer in the middle of the board and causes it to swell. That swelling displaces the lamination. Unrepaired surfboards separate the glass layer from the foam and become delaminated. On a board, it feels squishy. It seems benign. It is not. Delamination is cancer. Fix dings as they happen. Suck out the saltwater venom from the wound. Put your mouth over the hole and suck out the salt water. Spit it out. Let the board dry out for as long as the hole was big. In other words, a tiny hole needs a few days. A big, gaping hole needs a few months. Ding repair is beyond the scope or intention of this book. Little dings are easy. Big jobs need a pro. Don't fuck up that seven-hundred dollar board you bought if you are unsure about the degree of damage. Pay a pro to fix it. Don't put stickers, duct tape, wax, glue, or anything else on dings. It won't work. Water still gets in. Get it fixed, dammit. If you must fix one, let the board dry all the way out. Put your mouth over the ding and suck. Did you get any saltwater? If yes, let it sit. If no, you can fix it. Any ding bigger than a quarter is dicey, take it in. If not, remove any and all debris and wax from ding area. Use fine grade sandpaper to sand around the ding. Apply the proper epoxy to ding area and cover with a piece of clear wrap the size of the glued area. Allow it to dry. Remove plastic wrap from ding and sand it smooth. Some dings require glass. Take it to a pro, bro. You can try to do patchwork as a kook but I wouldn't recommend it on a new board. If you own a beater board or garage sale special, knock yourself out. New boards are like new cars. Take it to the shop. Stay away from stick-on tail guards, board length traction pads, and large stickers or spray traction. Nose guards are a wise purchase but not necessary. Don't add weight to your boards for fashion. Think function, not fashion. Your board needs to be as light as possible. Wax regularly by placing your board deck side up in blazing sunlight to melt old wax. Scrape it off and put on a fresh coat. That ball of old wax will tell you how much weight wax adds to your board. Every ounce matters. Don't add stuff that adds weight to your boards in the name of fashion. Keep it functional. Traction pads are for short boards. Forget about them for now. If you are driving to surf or are traveling to remote beaches, you need a waterproof container for wet shorts or your wetsuit. You should throw two extra towels in your car. Why two? Because sometimes you will need more than one towel to dry off. You will need to stand on one towel and dry off with the other. Put a good First-Aid Kit in your car. You are going to get cuts. Count on it. Keep extra wax in your trunk out of the sun. When you keep extra surf wax in your car, keep it out of the sun. It melts inside the packaging and changes the chemical make-up

and consistency of the wax. You
might also want to put an extra
change of socks, shoes, sweats, and
have a reliable cell phone. You will
want bigger clothes for after surf
sessions. They are easier to put on.
Salt water makes you sticky. The
other key item for your car is a water
bottle for before and after sessions.
Stay hydrated. Salt water wears out
your kidneys. It makes them retain
water. Drink tons of water an hour
before surfing. You also need a way
to hide your car keys while you're in
the water. If you own a truck, they
make hitch key safes. If you have a
car or van, get a magnetic key hider.
Bikes and motorcycles can be fitted
with surfboard racks. There are
wheeled carts for longboards to help
you get them to the beach for sale,
bring locks for those. Look around
before stashing your key! Surfer-
Thieves love kooks. Don't think
surfing at the rich beach will make
you immune to theft. Hide your keys
well. But, if you plan on being in the
water until dusk, don't hide them too
well! I got out at dusk and it got dark
fast. I had stashed my keys in the

bushes and almost couldn't find them because I couldn't see! I also suggest keeping snacks in your car. Sometimes the ocean drags you far away from where you got in. It may take hours to walk back. Having a snack could mean spiking your blood sugar at a much needed time. If you get into a dangerous situation and are in the water for hours until you get out, that snack could be a lifesaver. Other surfers will ask you for wax, water, ding epoxy, snacks, band-aids, and for a towel. Have extras in the car and you might make a friend. You may also want to keep a small tent in your car. I went surfing and my battery drained. Luckily, I had snacks, water, and a tent to sleep in. I had no cell phone signal and had to hike to the ranger's station the next day. Keep supplies in your car for surf adventures. You will be so glad you did if you get stranded. Keep jumper cables in your car, a full gas can, and back up battery. Other surfers may need help in remote surf spots. Its nice to lend a hand. Good karma.

2. Wetsuit or shorts? Again, where do you live? What is the water temperature? If you don't know, look online or stick your hand in the water. If you can't look online, watch local surfers. Are they wearing wetsuits? Are they wearing shorts? Are they wearing a short wetsuit or something else? Wear what they wear. If you aren't around people, go by water temperature. For example, northern California is frigid, year round. We wear wetsuits that are 4/3's. They are four millimeters in most places on the suit. However, in southern California in the dead of winter and spring, they wear 3/2's. If the water is warm or hot, boardshorts that cover the knees are the right choice. Wear a t-shirt or what's called a rashguard to avoid chafing on your chest. Chafing is a carpet burn-like wound that will definitely happen if you surf bare chested. Over time, one might develop a tolerance to shirtless surfing but my guess is that takes years. I got chafed so bad surfing in the Caribbean that I couldn't wear a shirt. My nipples were on fire, as

were the several rub raw spots on my chest. Yeouch! Don't try to look cool by going shirtless. You will moan in regret after you get out of the water. If you want to build up to surfing shirtless, good luck. It hurts and takes a long time but you can get calloused. Wear boots and a neoprene head covering cap if you are in the cold. Surfing barefooted is fine until you get skegged on the ankle. Then, you will wish you had boots on. If you are in warm water, forget about boots. If you are in cold water, wear boots. Being cool by letting your feet get numb, just to be the odd man out makes you look like what you are for resisting logic: a kooky douchebag. There are some surfers who denounce boots. Good for them. They can enjoy being badass. I will cover as much skin as possible in cold water surf spots. After having been struck countless times by my board and its razor sharp fins, I prefer giving my skin a protective barrier. The wetsuit can prevent injury. If you are in cold water, you will relish being in your suit of armor but know it can be

penetrated. If you are just wearing
boardshorts, make sure they cover
your knees. Otherwise, they will get
chafed. When shopping for wetsuits,
get the cheapest one. Stay away
from wetsuits that feature an inner
lining that pulls up to cover your back
along where the zipper goes up.
They are a pain in the ass to reach if
you don't get them right when pulling
the suit up and on. Stay away from
wetsuits with sewn in hoods. As soon
as you go underwater and resurface,
there goes your hearing. Wetsuits
with zip out hoods are the same. Buy
a separate neoprene head cover
with a long bill to shield your eyes
from direct sunlight. Poke holes in
the ears so water drains out and you
retain your hearing. It may be "cool"
to have a built in hood and surf with
it, etc. I think it is never worth it to
lose your hearing. I also don't
recommend ear plugs for the same
reason. If you develop otitis, I'll be
impressed. You'd have to outsurf
most surfers to get that type of ear
damage. Wetsuits are a pain in the
ass to put on. Try one foot, then, the
other. Grab the suit and go over your

calves, knees, thighs and crotch. Stop. Insert one arm until your hand makes it through. Then, do the other arm. Reach behind you and feel for the zipper. Pull it up. Try to find wetsuits that feature a piece of velcro that stops the zipper from coming down. If you are having trouble finding the right size, try the sizing chart on the tag. If that fails, ask a sales person to fit you for one. They will try to convince you to get that suit that fits great that you can't afford. Don't. You will end up with dozens of wetsuits. They all wear out the same. I have dropped hundreds and dropped a hundred and gotten similar results. If you surf a lot, you go through suits faster. But, once you acquire enough suits, you don't have to keep buying them. Don't buy boots with straps across the tops or back. You don't need those. Get the split toe slip ons without straps of any kind. Buckles from straps eat into your feet on hard turns. If they only carry boots with straps, cut them off. You don't need them. If you can't get your wetsuit on put a plastic grocery bag over your foot and try.

The bag will slide right through the suit's foothole. Once your foot is through, fish the bag through. Put it on the other foot. If you have to, you can do the same thing with your arms. Wetsuits will stretch some with use. But, you want it to be water tight. If the suit is letting in water, it is the wrong size. If you are so restricted by the suit that you fear tearing it, it is the wrong size. Go back. Swap it. Hurry. When hanging your suit up after a session, keep it out of direct sunlight. It will melt the collar on some suits which leaves a black smudge on your skin that has to be scrubbed off. If you don't rinse your wetsuit after each use with fresh water, you will ruin it. Rinse it out and hang it up. Drive a nail somewhere in your shower area to hang it up. Use a plastic hanger. Metal hangers leave a residue and rust. Don't buy or wear gloves in the water. Gloves create too much drag. Don't buy wetsuits online. You need to try it on.

3. Wax: where do you live? Is the water at the beach you surf warm or cold? The answers to those questions will

determine what type of wax you will need, buy, and use. If you are buying wax in a hot climate, where the water temperature is hot or warm, you need SexWax warm water formula or a market equivalent. If you are in cold water, like us surfers in northern California, you need two kinds of wax: a base coat and cold water wax. Read the label on the wax. They all say what conditions they are formulated for. You must wax correctly. Failure to do so will result in serious injury. No shit. Waxing your board is critical and an art form. It will take time to get it right. You start diagonally left and go all the way down the board making diagonal stripes of wax, then you go diagonal right. The goal is to leave diamond shaped criss-crosses of wax all along the top or deck of your board. Those form the basis of bumps of wax you create by coming back and forth, horizontally. Put the joint down and picture this: you are using the wax to build little bumps to grip into. The way to do it is by going diagonal left, from top to bottom, now, come back right, diagonally.

Stop and look. See the diamonds? Now, come back and forth, from top to bottom. See the little bumps? Now, go back and forth, from top to bottom, again. They get taller and more plentiful. Put a good bit of wax on. And, bring it to the beach. How do you know when there's not enough wax? When you slip and do a face plant. Your goal is to create bumps that add traction on an otherwise glass-slick surface. Failure to wax correctly will get you injured. Ask for help. If no one is around, read my steps carefully. Don't get wax on the rails of the board. The rails are the sides. Wax all the way up, 3/4 of the board. Wax past where your chest makes contact. Or, you will slide off over and over. Don't wax the bottom, tip, rails, or fins- Dumbass. Wax the top of the board everywhere your body touches it. I get made fun of for waxing so much of my board but here I need it for grip. Ocean Beach likes to strip your board from you like an NFL tackler. Having enough wax on more of my board allows me to snatch it back in time crunch situations where I'm obligated to move out of another rider's way. You'll see.

4. Paddling- Surfing is 99% paddling. You will spends hours paddling and seconds riding. There is no way around it. Accept that paddling will comprise most of your session. Paddling is not for beginners. In the first year, you will be walking out to waist or chest high waves ONLY and turning and catching white water rides and practicing getting to your feet. Do not expect surfing to come easy or naturally, it won't. It requires extreme patience, diligence, determination, addiction, and obsession. On flat days (days where there are no waves) or if you can get to a lake, start practicing paddling. Paddling effectively means you are lying on your board most of the way up it while arching your back, WITH YOUR FEET TOGETHER at all times. You are creating a planing surface, that is you MUST position yourself in such a way that the nose of your board is elevated, just so, out of the water. If you are paddling and your board's front end is submerged, scoot back. If you are too far back,

your board will stick up too far out of the water and you will kill your arms trying to counter the drag from your tail and legs weighing the board down too deep in the water. Find the sweet spot on your board. Your strokes should be non-stop. That is, you power that board, at all times. Paddle by doing a swimmer's stroke. If you can't swim, never surf. Surfing for non-swimmers is a horrible, deathwish idea. If you can't swim, the ocean is no place to be. Stop reading now and take six months of swim lessons from a pro. Don't worry, I will wait. Keep your shoulders rigidly fixed. The rocking motion from loose shoulders creates drag when you are paddling. Your shoulder muscles, as they power your strokes, should be relaxed. Let your arms do the bulk of the work. If your board is rocking side to side as you're paddling, you're not doing it right. Revisit the board and just keep at it, consciously deciding to focus on not moving your shoulders and rocking the board. You are creating a planing surface. Remember that. Any unsmooth motion or jerkiness

<u>translates</u> <u>into</u> <u>added</u> <u>drag</u>. If you are a fat ass like me, your gut can be a nice fulcrum, of sorts. So, balance your center in the center that creates the least amount of drag and the most amount of planing speed. Paddling takes years to master. If you don't think it will, you're wrong. Watch the guys who rip the best. Paddling looks easy. That's because they are smooth, refined machines powering their boards effectively by creating a speedy planing surface and making their body a smoothly running rigid motor. Water is not easy to navigate in for the out of shape. Paddling takes years and can only be mastered by paddling all the time. Like I said in the beginning, if you can't commit to surfing all the time, don't start. Seriously. Find another hobby. Surfing requires paddlers who can act, move, and respond in the blink of an eye. Ask anybody who has collided with another surfer. Chances are, the collision happened so fast it was just like a car accident. I literally nearly killed a dude at Bolinas, a mellow beach, because he couldn't motor

out of the way fast enough. I tried to bail, it was too late. His head could have been impaled on the tip of my board. No shit. Thankfully, he just barely avoided death by ducking underwater. You beginners are deadly in the water when you are uninformed. That's why I'm telling you to forget about paddling, at first. Stay out of everybody's way, for the first year. And, just keep it simple: walk out with your board to your side, NEVER between you and the ocean, it WILL HIT YOU. Never turn your back to the ocean. **Find waves that are pushing all the way through to the shore. Make sure they are little, like no higher than your waist or chest and crumbling over, gently. Stay away from waves that collapse in big sections. They are called close-outs. They are not ridable. Riding any wave taller than you is rolling the dice on your health. Turn around when a waist high one is coming. Put your board down in it, just as it is approaching you. Keep the nose up by arching your back! Jump onto your board and**

ride it on your stomach with your feet together, back arched. Try to stand up, without going to your knees first. Ride the wave all the way in, repeat until exhaustion. Do that as many days out of the week for as long as you can. I guarantee you success. You must learn how to ride on your stomach and pop-up before anything else. You haven't even thought about duckdiving waves, placement of yourself and your board to catch waves, real paddling, and big waves. So, forget about those things until you have mastered the simple steps: picking a mellow day, walking out into waves no bigger than chest high, turning around with your board, placing it then yourself on it as the wave approaches then riding prone with your back arched until you can pop-up without going to a knee first. Until you have repeated that routine hundreds of times, you cannot move to the next level. The other critical requirement for my method is your Surf Journal. From now on, you will keep a four sentence per entry journal of every surf session you have. Why? Because, over time, you will learn from yourself what you are doing wrong and how to improve. The Surf Journal is written proof of progress. Each of the four sentences should detail the rides you got that day, praise or critique of said rides, and any other information about the learning to surf process. Keeping a Surf Journal sets my method apart from all others. It is our secret weapon. If you don't journal, you won't get the same results. Trust me. You need to log your experience. After hundreds of entries, you will see what I mean. You can literally pin point when you started getting better. Neglect the journal and you're a lazy kook. I can't wait for my students to come to my book signings and show me their Surf Journals. They will excel in their learning process much faster than the cut-corners kooks. If you can, film yourself surfing. That will also accelerate your learning process. Watch session videos closely. Are you coming to a knee or tripoding? Are you keeping your feet together when paddling or riding prone? Is your back arched? Aro you placing yourself on the board far up enough to minimize drag and create a planing surface? Are you rocking your shoulders when paddling? Are you turning the board with your hands not your hips when riding? Are you bailing off your board dangerously at the end of your rides? Do you look like a kook in the water due to flopping and flailing around too much? Does it look like you know what you're doing in the video? Are your feet spaced correctly once up and riding a wave? Do you have the correct gear for the beach you are surfing? Until your surfing looks as fluid and natural as everyone else's, keep filming and journaling. Those who don't will learn a lot slower. Surf Journal entries should include: the date of the session, the session number, and four sentences about the session. Keep your personal and professional life out of your journal entries. This journal is for process learning, not venting. If you write short, choppy sentences expect journaling to be useless. You obviously don't see its value and are shortchanging yourself not me or the method I'm prescribing. Write about your session. Pose questions. Give yourself props for good things, critique for bad habits. If you keep at it, you will die laughing at the early, primitive entries because you will see, on paper, your progress. And, you will know exactly how many times you have been surfing. Trust me. The Surf Journal is mandatory. All changes in life require a written contract, this is yours to surfing. You will dread it on shitty days after unproductive sessions. But, on good days, you will run to it to jot down your session highlights. Some entries will be longer than four sentences for that reason. Always find four sentences worth of useful information for your journal. Skimpy entries do no good. Get detailed and watch your learning curve explode over the other folks who bought all the other how-to surf manuals. The Surf Journal works. It is fail-proof. All it needs is you.

5. The Pop-Up: the most critical skill to successful surfing is the pop-up. It is as simple as gripping your board

around your chest area, on the sides, and in one smooth motion, getting to your feet. The problem is twofold: you will try going to a knee first and no matter how much you practice popping up, you will still blow it sometimes. Tripoding by going to your knee or placing a hand to steady yourself is the worst habit one can develop. I broke my hand playing football and was out of the water for months. When I started back, I had to consciously break myself of the habit of going to a knee first before standing up. You have to relearn surf skills. That is why you have to surf every single day that you can and never flake or drop off, ever. If you do, popping up will be your worst enemy. Repetition is the mother of skill but surf skills fade fast. That's why some local assholes are so bitter. They can't surf as much as they'd like so they take it out on you when you ask dumb questions or get in the way. Surfing is an addiction that demands obsessive behavior. You have to have a few screws loose to handle it. It will make you madder than anything in the world when you see a perfect wave coming and you can't get to your feet. I don't care who you are: mellow hippy longboarder or short boarding jock, not popping up correctly and missing waves is a recipe for extreme anger. Popping up is like the motion in a squat thrust: smooth, fluid, natural, and knee-free! Practice the popping up motion by practicing the squat thrust. Taking drops on your stomach and standing up is kooktacular but you will soon discover that that is cutting corners and not being true to the art of our sport. You need to get up, instantly, in order to maximize your time on the wave. Taking drops on your stomach and scrambling to your feet is lame. Unless you don't mind being thought of as a tool, pop-up as soon as the wave is under you. I have seen kooks practicing pop-ups on the beach on their boards. Don't bother. Just ride little crappy waves and practice popping up, as you are moving forward. The problem with practicing on the beach is that you are practicing on the beach, not in the water. The water changes everything.

6. Riding waves- the beginning year will be all about riding simple waves and popping up. You can paddle around on mellow days, too. And please practice paddling into small, safe, crumbly waves. You need to learn paddling then popping up on easy days. When you hop on your board, on your stomach, to ride something the goal is to get up on your feet as soon as possible. If you are cruising along, hesitating to stand up, don't! Get your butt up and ride. Riding on your stomach is like a heroin addict tying off an arm and not sticking the needle in. You can't get hooked on heroin if it doesn't get in your bloodstream and brain. Same thing with surfing: tie your arm off, stick the needle in, and push the plunger. Get off and get hooked. If you don't or you flake out, then you suck. Surfing is the best rush in the world. But, you won't find out riding on your stomach. Buy a body board if you want stomach rides. Riding waves, for the first year, will be straight rides to the shore and then you walk back

out and do it all over again. Oh, by the way, riding ALL the way up to the sand is not a good idea, your fins will get sheared off. So, bail before it gets that shallow. When you bail, bail to one side. Some dumb asses will bail in front of their board or between it and a wave, both hold disastrous outcomes. Your board is the deadliest thing in the water. Every injury I have had is related to the board striking me or my bashing into the board. Ask around. Any surfer worth his salt will tell you, the biggest danger is NOT the wave, its your board. The fins will cut you to the quick. I have slashes all over every wetsuit I own, evidence that skegging happens. If you are in a hot climate, barefooted, and in board shorts, I pity you when you get skegged. It hurts bad. I sliced my palm vertically in 2005. It was from grabbing at my board's tail. Don't do that. Those fins will fuck you up. Grab anywhere but the tail when you are snatching your board up. Another major rule: hold onto your board, AT ALL TIMES. Never ever lose grip. That board is your responsibility and liability. I recommend never ever getting off of your board or tooling around when there's other surfers in the water. Its annoying, not cute, and inconsiderate and the first thought everybody has is, " Look at the kook." So, don't float around in the water near your board or let it go anywhere without at least one hand firmly gripping it. If no one is around do whatever. Surf naked. I'm just talking about surf spots with more than just you there. Why am I such a hard ass about this? Because things happen so fast. If you have ever been in a car accident, you know what I mean. That board is a vehicle. It can save your life or end it. It can hurt somebody's kid or split their skull in half. Surfboards are as deadly as the dude riding them. If you are inconsiderate, a dick, or a kook with your board, something bad WILL happen to you, at some point. Don't risk it, control your board AT ALL TIMES. Now, once you have taken that to practice, you must get into snatching your board back after rides are over, as quick as you can. If you happen to get a wave and cruise it a long way for a long time, great! Once you bail, away from your board, be uber responsible and snatch it right back into your possession and control. Locals will appreciate and notice that good habit, and your other good habit of staying out of the way, and your other good habit of popping up without a knee contacting the board. Dude, this is how it must be, in the beginning. Things will change and development is directly proportionate to time put into surfing. Getting in the water and working your ass off, obsessively, without stopping, until you HAVE to end the session, every chance you get has a payday. My friend likes to go twice a day. I go at least four or five days a week. Surfing is a life changing addiction. It is as fatal as all other addictions. But, you cannot say no to good waves once you have had a taste. Imagine walking into a warehouse party where every single ideal beauty you can dream up is there and you can party with any one of them as hard and as nasty as you'd like. That is surfing. It is an orgy of joy. I literally crave it. You will, too. But, not if you flake or excuse yourself from its rigorous ways all the time. Stop being that way. Its just depression. Face it and break it by surfing. It will save your life. You will find peace and solace on the ocean's infinite faces. You will be unburdened, free of worry. You will experience the only sensation comparable to winged flight. You will zip down the line and the smile and cheers will awaken your soul. Surfing heals the sad dudes. Ask them. They will all swear by their Mother. I do. So, anyway, don't bail on yourself once you start surfing. Let that joy permeate all facets of your life. Riding waves starts with riding straight, just like you've been doing, this whole time, right? If you haven't been practicing for a solid year catching small waves, first, stop reading. The next part of the book is the next level, you're still a kook but you are earning your stripes by: displaying considerate, well-informed practices, maintaining control of your board, staying sober during the first year while surfing, (I know you are going to blaze one and think to go jump in, if you do, be careful. For example, California pot slows you down) working diligently on paddling with no drag, working on popping up to your feet without tripoding as soon as the wave gets you, and riding waves straight to the shore. You get mad every once in a while when you see the veterans, way out there, shredding waves. But, you stay on the inside. Going out there before putting time in is a dangerous mistake. It would be like walking on to an NFL team because you ran the ball up and down the field while no one was there. You will be regarded as a danger and a nuisance. Those guys will eat you alive. Ladies? This is where your disadvantage comes into play. That boyfriend or love interest who is teaching you will want you to stay by them and paddle out, etc. Don't exceed your comfort level to preserve his ego. If you don't feel comfortable out there, hang out on the inside, near the shore. Guys who teach their girlfriends are a nuisance and a danger to those of us who have to keep a constant eye on when he pressures her into trying a wave she's scared of. We all hold our breath hoping she resurfaces, injury free. Too many times these dudes have pressured their ladies into gnarly waves and they've gotten hurt, bad. Ladies? Don't let some surf guru tell you you will be fine if you are afraid. Just go with your gut. There are women who RIP hardcore all over the world. Watch Sofia Mulanovich. Case in point. Women have as much right to be out there as any guy alive. Some guys either hit on girls or block them out of waves. Both are sexist and repugnant. Those guys are the same ones at the bar that act that way to women. They suck. Don't let them bully you or scare you from learning how to surf. Don't let them disrespect you. Be ready to have at least one guy every few sessions who either gets in your way, glares at you, or hits on you. Surfing attracts all kinds of guys but most of us are jerks. I am. But, I'm trying to improve. At my worst, I have never bugged a girl in the water or taught a girl just to impress or endear myself to them but I have been annoyed with guys forcing girls into dangerous situations around other surfers, just to toot their own horns. Ladies, I love each and everyone of you. This book has you in mind, too. So, hang out and learn more. You rock, all of you. You are all the mothers of our kind. Don't let some surf bum take your dignity. Tell them to kiss both sides of your ass if they tell you to leave or get out of their way. You have as much right to be there as they do, this is 2011.

Chapter 2- Surfing from paddling into waves and duck diving.

The next phase of surfing is turning the board. You have now been getting in at your local beginner beach and have mastered catching and standing up on waves and riding them to the shore. Yay. Good job. Insert pat on the back. Now, let's turn the damn thing!

So, you have been curious and perhaps even happened upon turning on one of your many slowed down, small scale rides over the last twelve months. You may have noticed those placements of your feet that made for the best ride. Chances are, they were spread out and dug in, effectively giving your toes and heals the run of the deck. Well, that's how you turn. You dig in the direction you want the board to go. Turn with your hips to match the speed of the wave. Don't turn by telegraphing with your hands or swinging your torso, you don't have to. Settle down, Beavis. Just dig toes to get down and in front and dig heals to go with your back to the wave. Most of the time, at this stage, you will be bearing down on your toes to turn. Focus on how your hips alter the turn.

Get a feel for that. If you bought a hybrid or longboard like you were supposed to, then turning will telegraph easier throughout the board. If you were stubborn and got a short board, you will have a lot of trial and error learning. You can eventually do it, just be ready to bust your ass to get there. I was you. I bought a shortboard first. Dumb decision. But it was all I could afford thanks to graduate school. As soon as I bought my 7'10 Maricio Gil board, dubbed Bobby, after saying "dang it bobby" from King of the Hill at first when he would make me miss waves, I was able to excel. You really need a template in your head for surfing built upon riding a hybrid. Just get one. Don't get a god damn soft top, for god's sake, I'm not pulling out that soapbox again. You need to spend time paddling around and laying the foundation for duck diving.

The art and necessity of duck diving:

Goal: get you and the board under water before that incoming wave buries you. Execution: depends on board size, don't try ducking long boards or do that turtle roll move where you go upside down under it. So stupid. Inefficient and screams kook. Just push down as the white wash hits you, bury the nose. Yes, you will get washed back. Yes, it will drive you nuts. But, longboarders should maximize their boards buoyancy and paddle like hell to get out to the peaks they want. Duck diving a gun is as easy as it gets, as far as I'm concerned. Wide longboards fair better getting shoved not ducked. The longboard rider should focus on paddling out, not getting under waves. Some beaches are structured in such way as to permit passage that way. My guess is that it takes years to learn how to execute effectively and you aren't there yet. So, if you have a longboard, takes the hits. If you bought a hybrid you can corkscrew duck dive. It takes years to learn. You plunge the tip of the nose in as you are submerging and twist the board under the whitewash. As you will soon discover, duck diving is the marriage of timing and execution under a falling face. Watch other guys do it. Mimic them. You will get it wrong all the time while learning. Sometimes you will duck dive, over and over and be paddling and you still can't paddle out far enough to ride. Duck diving means to grab the top of your board and submerge it and you, down and at an downward angle, to avoid getting walloped by a broken wave's monster white wash. Watch the veterans of your break. Copy their method. Some stick out a stiff leg, some dolphin through the walls, like they were born there, some twist the nose as they angle in, some get the timing wrong and get worked. Duck diving takes years. It will be the arrow in your quiver you need most to slay the dragon so don't neglect working on it. You will eventually develop your own style. Duck diving shorter boards is much easier. The trade off is paddling a shorter board wears you out faster. Pick your poison. They both taste bittersweet. Duck diving is also very dangerous if done too early or too late. As you did with the waves before, start small. Don't bite off more than you can chew. You will get spit out on your face. And, you will drink deeply from the ocean's infinite salty bosom. Duck diving is all timing and timing is all about having a trained eye for when to duck. You cannot develop into a duck diver until you have surpassed the joy of riding straight to the beach over and over. You will be paddling and duck diving more and more. Don't worry, everybody sucks at it for years in the beginning. Let a solid three years of practice get under your belt and you will start to see how critical duck diving is to surfing with any degree of advancement. You cannot progress without paddling and duck diving being daily staples that comprise the vast majority of your session hours. It is an inescapable reality of surfing. Nothing in life is free, including riding waves. You have to work for it and want it. There will be plenty of days where you will do nothing but duck diving and paddling. Trust me. Even the golf pro has bad games. Surfing is the same way. The ocean is a dictator. You don't get a vote. You happen upon waves or you do not. Duck diving opens the door to advanced surfing. It is the only way you will reach the peaks that will hone your riding skills. Guys who can't duck dive are at a major loss. Don't let laziness or delusions convince you to avoid the two. They are the crux and backbone of surfing: duck diving and paddling. Without them in your repertoire you won't be able to excel. So, good news for those of you who are reading who like surfing the way it is for you now, you may put the book down, you're finished. But, for those of you who want to go further: heed my warning. You will suffer under the scepter of the duck diving and paddling Gods. Kneel before them and they may grant you access to paradise.

Chapter 3- Wave types and selections

1. The Close-out-- this annoying buzz
   kill is easy to spot: a wave coming
   pitches up and violently dumps over
   too fast to mount. Close-outs do
   what they say: close out. If you can't
   spot a close-out, don't surf. Waves
   that close out chop you in half. They
   are the most dangerous and
   impossible to ride. They can break
   your back or your board. Leave them
   alone. If you see a wave that falls, all
   at once, with an audible thud, and a
   slamming guillotine-like motion, that
   is a close-out. Don't get in, if you
   braved it and didn't know, get out or
   pay dearly.
2. The Crumbler- this is a wave that
   crumbles over and creates a ridable
   face. Crumblers peel left or right.
   They are safe, fun, and fertile
   learning ground for you. Crumblers
   fall safely and are characterized by a
   feathering top that gives way to a
   ridable face. Crumblers are your
   friend. I light up upon seeing them.
   At my beach, which is among the
   most dangerous in the world, I am
   into safe, fun, productive sessions. I

recommend adopting that position. Don't try to impress anyone.

3. Barrels or tubes- Good luck, if you can get one to yourself. If you are in a place with tubes and barreling waves, good luck trying to get one, at all. Great waves are never left alone these days. If you happen upon tubing waves and no one is around, you must understand that the lip of that peeling wave you are trying to get covered up with is a lot heavier than you think. Getting barreled is for experts or advanced surfers. If you stumble into some wave paradise, get your fill. I envy you. Chances are this will not occur. Tubing waves are the porn of the surf experience and if you get them, you are the star. Keep in mind that barrel will clip you, dump you, tumble you, and deceive you. If you can get into tubes after reading this book, I will bend over and kiss my own ass. I feel that tube riding is beyond the scope of my rudimentary guide and hereby refer you out to other books and videos, maybe even a pro instructor.

4. Big waves- You have no business being in any wave over your head or slightly over your head, without at least five solid years of surfing under your belt. I hereby refer you to private instruction as I do not wish to receive an email from your widow stating that you read my book section on big wave riding and decided to go for it and croaked. No thanks. I have surfed some of the biggest waves of winter, at Ocean Beach, here in San Francisco. It was a culmination of years and years of conditioning and terrifying errors. Big waves are for experts. To be an expert, you must become one. I can't take you down that road. I am not Laird Hamilton. I am a sassy, Alabama-redneck, beachbum/former doctor turned surf Barney/Novelist. Big wave riding is the NFL of surfing. I am content with backyard football-guerrilla surfing of medium to large waves. Big waves are for the Gods. Watch the videos and drool.

5. The Hodge-Podge wave- this is a wave that has qualities of all above stated waves. My beach embodies the hodge-podge as it throws curve

balls and strikes or hits home runs, with eight arms, two of which are holding baseball bats! The hodge-podge wave starts as a crumbler, sections off into a close out, and criss-crosses to peak into a monster twice its original size! Hang on for dear life and try to anticipate where it will go next.

6. The ankle lapper- this is the baby of the bunch. These little guys are a recipe for fun, safe, peaceful longboarding or hybrid riding. These are what you should cut your teeth on. Seriously, the real surfers and veterans make surfing look easy. Neil Pert makes playing drums look easy but it is not. Sticking to small waves for your beginning years is fun, safe, and productive. All of those Matthew MacKinda-lames out there, far away from you, on their stand-up paddle boards and short boards talking to each other about obscure surf crap make it look easy because they worked for it. You may hate them. You may clown them. You may pine over their rejections. You may say you can do it better. But, if I were you, I would let that shit go. Surfing

speaks for itself, if you work and work, research, and strategically ask around, you can slip into surf culture and riding technique. But, most importantly, put the time in and you will reap the benefits.

Like everything else that looks easy that is done by a pro, it is because they put the time in. You cannot achieve the same results without consistent hard work. There is no substitute for years and years of diligent practice. Cut corners and flake on your surf diet or journal and you will notice your hatred of the veterans will burn brighter. Water extinguishes fire. Get your lazy ass off the couch and go surf more. That's why I won't tell you to try big waves and barrels. That's for those of us who have worked for years and years. Sometimes decades. You are not allowed into that world, yet. Pay your dues and we shall see. For now, seriously, just focus on surfing small, medium, and crumbling large waves, no bigger than your fast heartbeat tells you. When in doubt, get out. That is my rule of surfing. Waves that make you nervous are not at your service. Get out. Pull your ego out of your asshole and paddle in. Don't try to impress the unimpressable locals. Just survive. If you spend most of your session looking at other dudes and watching them rip, go back to riding the inside peaks. If you are hesitating in any waves, get out. Never ever turn your back to the ocean. Always stay facing the horizon. Sit up on your board, at all times. You can see better and further. Learn your beach. Know thyself. Combine the two and add a healthy dose of panic and use that as your litmus for wave quality. The tides will affect your waves, the season and winds will factor in, too. These are details I cannot provide. You must research your local beach. I know I said earlier veterans and locals should be avoided in the water and at the surf shop. I stand by that. Go to their local bar. Look for guys wearing surf shirts, hats, hoodies, or listen for them. Insert yourself into a conversation with the nicest sounding one, somehow. Or go online and ask questions in a forum, if you are shy. Just remember: you never know who you are getting advice from unless you have seen them shredding at your beach. BUT, if they talk over your head about surfing, have extensive beach knowledge of tides and seasonal changes in wave shape, size, and quality and seem to be an expert on most things related to surfing, tell them you are an annoying kook beginner and you don't want to piss anybody off. Then, ask how can you do whatever it is you need help with. The loud obnoxious friend standing next to them is to be avoided at all costs. He will shun you. He will smell kook on your breath. Buy him and the nice guy a beer but corner the nice guy to pick his brain. Buying drinks and flattery will get you everywhere. Be nice. Be yourself. Don't talk about surfing the whole time. Ask about music, ask about girls, ask about what they do for work. Drop your insecurity and soon you will be paddling next to one of those guys. When you do, don't worship them. But, don't get in their way either. Try not to talk too much when in the water. It is like someone coughing when you are about to putt in golf. Surfing is a sport. Treat the other surfer as you would on a golf course, with respectful silence. Hooting and hollering on a good day is great. Never stop doing that. Inane fodder conversation to cover up your social insecurity or to fill the silence is annoying and tinny on the ears. I paddle away from those motor mouth nice-guy kooks. I am NOT out here to chit-chat about the tide, the weather, the waves, etc. I came out here to work out. Do you run your mouth at the gym or on the golf course? I hope not. Don't mention my book if you do! Anyway, making friends who surf is slow. There are tons of perfectly nice dudes who rip who will gladly teach you and correct you. I am just a jaded redneck asshole with few friends. If you are friendly and outgoing by nature, you will meet plenty of surfer brethren. Alcohol is the only way I have made surf buddies. Otherwise, I want surfing all to myself. I want to wallow in it. I want to squander its gold and take treasure baths beneath its murky, sparkling waters. I want every face of every wave to stretch to shores where there are no men...with their greed and destruction. I want my surfing to be almost a sexual release, something private, like a secret flight taken only alone and never with another. Develop your dependence on the ocean and squander it. Fuck everybody else. The ridable waves will show themselves. If you are panicked, the waves are not for you, get out. Come back next time. Surfline.Com tells you wave heights in feet. Never go over five feet. After years and years of surfing, do what feels right. But, for now: stay away from waves that are five feet and up. I don't care if you are Samson and Hercules put together, you are not immortal. Drowning happens. Severe injury happens. But, most likely, you are going to get injured if you push yourself in waves that make you hesitant and/or nervous. Fear leads to error. When you panic, you become manic. Don't spoil the party that is your life just by trying to look cool. Get out when you are scared. Our brains are hard wired for three things: fucking, fighting, and surviving. Your body will let you know how to proceed, if you listen. If you ignore that pounding heartbeat because the local surf king has paddled out and he MUST see you ride, you are helpless and hopeless. When the paramedics ask you on the way to the hospital who taught you to surf don't utter my name! I told you here, right now, to not push your comfort level.

Panic is fatal. And, that brings us succinctly to chapter four!

Chapter 4- Ocean Survival

1. Panic is fatal. Read everything you can on the stories of people who survived severe circumstances and situations. They are alive because at some point they stopped panicking and started acting rationally. Example: I went out in December of 2005, two days before my birthday. I had been ripping on my shortboard. I got sucked out. Seven monster winter waves got me, in a row. I nearly drowned during the third and fourth waves. The fifth and sixth were hazy. The seventh was the godsend that washed me ashore. I collapsed on the beach. No one was in sight. When I got home, my lips were blue. Before doing anything else, I snatched out a piece of computer paper and sat on my front porch in my dripping wetsuit and jotted down my Will. It was that profound. I panicked that day. The Surf Gods spared me that day. I got lucky. I learned that big waves and panic make for certain death. That is why I warn of panic's lure. Your brain will go into panic mode in the ocean

faster than on land. You must tune in early to changes in your body. Here is what I ask myself: Are you cool, calm, and collected? I call it being 3-C'ed: cool, calm, collected. If you are not cool, you are hot. Meaning that you are burning up with fear and anxiety. If you are calm, you can answer the question quickly with a dismissive smirk. If you are not calm, you will hesitate to answer this question. If you are collected, each movement and expenditure of energy is efficient and moving you closer to your next ride. If you are not collected, you are all over the place. Get yourself together or get out. Being stubborn and panicky is a sure way to the grave or hospital. There is no one on the beach timing your session or watching you. Just leave if you are panicky. If you are a little nervous, monitor it. If you are panicking after a big wave snuck up on you, calm down. Control your breathing. Paddle out of there, fast. Get to shore. Come back another day. If you are surfing beyond your limits and you are panicking regularly one day, you will get hurt, bad. Taper back, don't push too hard. Come on, you know who you are. Stop rolling the dice. You may be fooling your buddies but you aren't fooling yourself. Why suffer? Panic sucks. Calm down or get out.

2. Panicky mindset leads to bad decisions. If you are panicky and in a dangerous situation in the water, either you chill out and think fast with logic or you let passion prevail. Guess who loses? Passion. Logic is the better choice. If someone is about to collide with you and they are the one who stole the ride from you, in the first place, get out of the way anyway. Why risk injury? There will be more waves. There will only and always be only one of you. Yes, the guy who burned you is an asshole but you let logic dictate your actions, not your anger at him for burning you on a wave. If you see a giant wave coming to take you out of this world and you panic, you will drown. Let it hit you and take you with it. Hold your breath and cover your head. Movement and struggle of any kind burns oxygen. Don't kick your legs and flail your arms if you

get taken under. Let it take you.
Waves usually won't keep you under
longer than thirty seconds.
Underwater, those thirty seconds feel
like eternity. Don't panic. Never ever
let go of your board, unless the
ocean will most certainly crush you
with it. If you are holding your board
in huge scary whitewash, it will
eventually resurface with you. I have
read about and experienced plenty
of near-death-experience sized
waves. I am alive and writing this
book because I turned off the panic
switch. Once you get to shore, you
can shit your shorts but NEVER
panic in the ocean. It sounds easy
and easily dismissible until
something really scary happens. If
you get sucked out to sea, paddle
parallel to the shore. Rip currents are
deadly. Find out how they manifest at
your beach. Panic is insidious,
dangerous, instant and your cue to
apply logic. If you succumb to panic
in the ocean, resolve it instantly or
perish. Remember: Lieutenant SAD,
(Lt. Sad) Live To Surf Another Day!
Panic will happen. Squash it then get

out of the ocean as quickly and efficiently as you can.

3. Other surfers up and riding have the right of way. If you see a guy up and riding, get out of his way. If he is going left, you go right. If he is going right, go left. If he is headed straight for you, bail at the last second and go under water and stay down. It is your job to stay away from all other surfers at all times. Crowds suck. But, they happen. Just know that you better fucking move fast or there will be Hell to pay. The number one reason veteran surfers hate beginners like you, is you get in the way. Please, dear God, don't get in other surfers way, ever. Go to extremes to avoid guys up and riding. Sometimes shit happens but most of the time, it was your fault for not moving fast enough to avoid collision with someone who has the right of way. Again: ANY surfer up first on a wave or heading towards you while you are paddling out has the right of way.

4. Assholes drop-in or steal waves from you on purpose. Veterans/locals will drop in on you because they can tell

by your sloppy paddling and that stupid grin on your face that you are a beginner. Advanced surfers will purposely try to flank you, beat you out of waves, drop in on you, and cut you off. Yes, its lame. Yes, they suck for doing it. But, nothing can stop the pecking order. Know your place. Get out of their way. Everytime. If you don't like it, don't surf when they're there. Go during business hours during the week. Weekends are a free-for-all. If you really want to surf, you have to have time in the water to learn how to paddle out of the way. Paddling out of the way requires fast, instantaneous response and keen attention to one's placement in the ocean in relation to the approaching rider. It is your job to move. But, when you are riding and some tool won't or can't move, just bail. Don't keep riding towards another person in the water who can't or won't move. Avoid collisions at all costs. Even if it means getting out and finding a peak down the beach that is unoccupied or has less dudes milking it.

5. Never ever bail off your board and swim for it. Duh! Your surfboard is a

life preserver, at the very least!
Resist the panic-fueled idea that you
should just swim for it. Keep your
board! If your leash breaks, swim
steadily for the shore. At the end of a
ride, don't shoot your board forward
out from under your feet as you're
bailing. It is inconsiderate and
stretches your leash.

6. Once up and riding a wave, know
   that other surfers may not see you
   and may try to get on your wave.
   Either bail or shout for them. I find
   shouting the word "Yo!" carries an
   innocuous meaning. It could mean,
   "Hey asshole, get off my wave!" or it
   could mean "Look out, its about to be
   a party wave!" Let them decide. If
   they drop in on you anyway, just bail.
   Avoid fights, arguments, and
   debating. Its not worth it. If some
   douche attacks you, gouge their
   eyes out for me. Surfing attracts
   major assholes and narcissists.
   They fly to the bright blue light and
   sizzle on the Lord Neptune's back
   porch. They are awful people, both
   onshore and off. If some shit head
   picks a fight with you, fight to the
   death. Some kook here was

strangled nearly to death a few years ago for fighting back against a group of idiot locals under the Golden Gate Bridge. They strangled him and left him floating face down in the water. I told you this sport is life or death. If you want something safe and easy, go to the gym. Surfing can include any lunatic who can ride a board. Avoid other surfers. If you must surf with them, stay away. Don't talk unless spoken to first. Don't try too hard. Just take your scraps and be grateful. Time will open the doors. Having a friend or a few friends that you surf with is the best case scenario. I prefer to surf alone but most normal people want a buddy to go with.

7. When in Rome... Imitate and follow the crowd. The best way to avoid conflict in crowds is to avoid crowds altogether, have a friend with you, buy a diver's dagger to wear on your ankle for self-defense, bail on waves other dudes drop in on even though you had it first, blend in with a crowd but hang out on the edges of it, or move to remote surf spots if you can't handle the crowd factors.

Otherwise, prepare for every surf session to challenge you with questions about the right of way of other surfers and your relation, spatially, to them and how to get out of their way and why you should, etc. People ruin everything, including surfing. I hesitated to write this book for that fact alone but I would rather you try this sport from an informed place instead of doing like I did which was to read one book and watch the endless summer movies. Surfing is awesome. But, if I had it to do over, I would want a book like this to save me the guesswork and inevitable embarrassment of not knowing the right-of-way rule. So, if you see another guy up and riding, get out of their way. Don't panic in the ocean, you will die. If you panic every time you surf, you are at the wrong beach. If you panic at the mellow beach, surfing ain't for you. And, if you read this and turn your life over to being a surfer, don't just read this. Read, watch, listen, practice, and absorb everything you can about your local surf breaks and culture. But, most of all, thank your

God for giving you the chance to
sing in the choir with the Angels.

Surfing was for kings only, in antiquity.
Thank goodness, the world has no
Kingdom, only nature. You have as
much right to be in the water as
anybody else. Enjoy!
And, please buy and read all of my
Novels for sharing this knowledge with
you. Come on! Help me get my fix. After
all, I tied off your arm and handed you
the loaded syringe.
Stick it in and push.
Let the liquid addiction take you over
and never forget what Jeff Spicoli said to
the wave, "Hey Bud! Let's Party!"

Dedication:

To Bethany Hamilton, the bravest surfer
I know...

To Stephen Morse, my surf teacher,
eternal guide, and friend. I miss you,
brother. Every wave I ride is for you.

And..let me not forget:

To Anthony Bourdain. This book is waiting for you on those days when you can finally kick back, smoke pot, and learn to surf. I love your show!

Printed in Great Britain
by Amazon